CLARE HARRIS

The Well

WITHDRAWN

D0326092

MACMILLAN

It is summer. The air is hot. It is hot inside Lia's house.

Lia lives with her mother, her father and her brother, Jay. Her grandmother lives with them too.

Lia's grandmother is old and sick. She lies in her bed all day. The old woman is sad. Her husband is dead. She often talks to his photograph.

Yes, husband? Oh, it's in the well. It's in a bucket of water. Thank you.

Lia and her mother are in Grandmother's room. Lia's mother brings some food and water.

'Please, go to the well,' says Grandmother. 'Bring me some water in the bucket.'

'There is no well here, Ma,' says Lia's mother. 'You live in the town now. We have good water. It comes from the tap.'

Lia's mother speaks quietly to her daughter.

'Grandmother is sick,' she says. 'She is not thinking clearly.'

Lia's mother gives the old woman some water.

'No, no,' says Grandmother. 'Go to the farm's well.'

'We must not visit the old farm now, Ma,' Lia's mother says. 'The farm is near the volcano. The volcano is dangerous. There is fire and smoke. Soldiers are guarding the roads.'

Grandmother doesn't hear her.

'Go to the well,' Grandmother says again. 'Bring me the bucket of water. Please hurry.'

'I'll go,' says Lia. 'I'll walk to the farm. I know the way.'

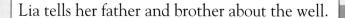

Lia tells her father and brother about the well.

Lia, you mustn't visit the farm. The volcano is near the farm. The volcano is dangerous.

I'll go with Lia. We'll get the water for Grandmother.

The next morning, Lia and Jay get up early.

Lia puts some bread and a sausage in her bag.
She puts a bottle of water in the bag too.

Jay and Lia are on the highway. The air is hot. The air is full of dust.

At the checkpoint, Lia and Jay meet a soldier. He talks to them. The volcano isn't dangerous today.

We're going to our grandmother's farm.

CHECKPOINT

She's sick. She wants water from the well. It will cure her sickness.

You're going to get some magic water? Bring me some too.

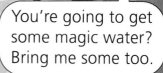

Lia and Jay stop next to a bridge. They eat their lunch.

There is a small house next to the bridge. A friendly woman lives there. She talks to Jay and Lia. She has a small dog. It is a small, red dog.

Jay gives the dog some sausage.

'Where are you going?' the woman asks. 'It is a hot day.'

'We're going to our grandmother's farm,' Jay replies. 'She is sick. She wants water from the well.'

9

Lia walks on. After a minute, Jay follows her. They walk and they walk. There are no houses here. There are no animals. There is dry grass and there is dust.

They hear a sound.

'What is that sound?' Jay asks. 'Is someone calling us?'

'No. It's the sound of the wind,' Lia replies.

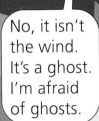

No, it isn't the wind. It's a ghost. I'm afraid of ghosts.

There are no ghosts here.

Lia and Jay are at the farm.

Jay sees oranges on a tree.
He doesn't see any ghosts.
He pulls some oranges from
the tree.

Lia and Jay find the well. Its cover is broken. Jay lifts the cover. The water doesn't smell good.

'Ugh! This water is bad, Lia,' Jay says.

'We must take some water for Grandmother,' Lia replies. 'We must get the bucket. We must pull this rope.'

They hold the rope.
They pull and they
pull. The bucket is
very heavy.

At last, the bucket
is out of the well.
It is full of dirty water.

Lia empties the
bucket.
Jay and Lia have a
surprise!

Gold! These
are gold coins!

Yes! I remember
these. They are
Grandfather's coins.

Lia and Jay are carrying the bucket. It is heavy. There are lots of oranges in the bucket. The gold coins are under the oranges.

Jay and Lia meet a gang of boys near the bridge.

'What's in your bucket?' the boys shout.

The small, red dog runs out of the house. He barks at the gang of boys. He barks and he barks.

The friendly woman comes out of the house. The boys run away.

Jay and Lia are at the checkpoint. The soldier looks in the bucket.

You don't have any magic water.

No. We have some magic oranges!

Lia and Jay give the soldier some oranges. The soldier smiles at them.

Lia and Jay are at home now. Their grandmother is lying in her bed.

Is that my bucket of water?

No! It's Grandfather's gold!

Everybody laughs. They are very happy. Grandmother looks at her husband's photo. She smiles.

Suddenly, they hear a sound. Is it the sound of the wind?